broken crayons
STILL COLOR

Overcomer

DEFEATING ANXIETY & ABUSE

iDisciple | Publishing

OVERCOMER

Published by iDisciple Publishing, 2555 Northwinds Parkway, Alpharetta, GA 30009.

Published by iDisciple Publishing, 2555 Northwinds Parkway, Alpharetta GA 30009.

ISBN: 978-0578920535

Cover and layout design by Annabelle Grobler

broken crayons
STILL COLOR

Overcomer

DEFEATING ANXIETY & ABUSE

20-Day Devotional Study for Women

TONI COLLIER · SEWA FIELDS
HOPE MOQUIN · NATHALIE MAXEY

Summary

Defeating Abuse/Abusive Cycles

Overcoming that "trapped" and "labeled" feeling

Worth: Your worth isn't tied to how you have been treated

There is still hope to be fought for and reached for.

There is no darkness Jesus can't touch, and there is no pain we can't come back from. We cannot be defeated. We are overcomers.

1

VICTIMS HAVE WORTH, IT NEVER LEFT.

TONI COLLIER

The Lord is a refuge for the oppressed,
a stronghold in times of trouble. Those who
know your name trust in you, for you Lord,
have never forsaken those who seek you.

PSALM 9:9-10 (NIV)

¹ I will give thanks to you, Lord, with all my heart;
I will tell of all your wonderful deeds.
² I will be glad and rejoice in you;
I will sing the praises of your name, O Most High.
³ My enemies turn back;
they stumble and perish before you.
⁴ For you have upheld my right and my cause,
sitting enthroned as the righteous judge.
⁵ You have rebuked the nations and destroyed the wicked;
you have blotted out their name for ever and ever.
⁶ Endless ruin has overtaken my enemies,

you have uprooted their cities;
even the memory of them has perished.
⁷ The Lord reigns forever;
he has established his throne for judgment.
⁸ He rules the world in righteousness
and judges the peoples with equity.
⁹ The Lord is a refuge for the oppressed,
a stronghold in times of trouble.
¹⁰ Those who know your name trust in you,
for you, Lord, have never forsaken those who seek you.

PSALM 9:1-10 (NIV)

I remember the first time I was abused. I felt utterly taken advantage of, dishonored and worthless. It was as if my worth and desire for dignity had simply numbed, vanished even. I wasn't worth the respect of a man anymore or even friends. I was no longer in need of soft, kind words and the patience and strength that it takes to restrain yourself from crossing a boundary in someone's life. I was now a punching bag, a victim, never to be redeemed and surely never to be honored. And isn't that what being an abuse victim feels like? Like maybe the life we once prayed for is

out of reach, not because of something we've done, but something that was done to us. Like we've been permanently etched with the badge "abused" even if we hadn't told a soul. Our hearts know. Our hearts remember the pain.

And you know who else remembers the pain? Our Heavenly Father does. Often times when we are in an abusive situation or circumstance, we hide and isolate because of shame. We forget or simply don't know the words that David writes in

Psalm 9:9, (ESV). That, "The Lord is a stronghold for the oppressed, a stronghold in times of trouble." God really does have our backs; He really is a pillar of strength when we have none. And not only that, but He sees you when you're in trouble, when you've been oppressed and abused and when your worth feels like it's numb. The hard part is believing that.

Whether your abuse has been at the hands of a man, a woman, a leader or a parent, please don't

allow that experience to take the truth away from you. And, the truth is, you do have a Heavenly Father that sees you and knows the pain you've walked through. He's also given you a worth that just can't be erased. I know all of this sounds fluffy or simply untrue when you're in the middle of the pain of abuse. Maybe you've completely doubted that there is a God, because if there were He wouldn't let this happen to you. Don't let abuse

sow that lie into you. There is a God that's weeping with you and sorrowful over the darkness in our world. And, He's surely not happy this has happened to you.

Hold on to the promises of Psalm 9:9, daughter of the King. God is a pillar of strength for you; He always has been.

PRAYER FOR TODAY

Pray this prayer today; God, thank you for being my stronghold. Right here in this season of hurt, confusion and pain, you are here. And even when my flesh feels weak and I feel calone, will you help me trust that you're with me? Will you remind me that just as you were with David while writing the book of Psalms, reminding us all that you're our stronghold, you are here now with me as well. God, open my heart to trust you, to allow you into the deep places of grief and sorrow and shame that I can carry because of what has happened to me. In Jesus' name, amen.

2

HE'LL THROW YOU A PARTY.

TONI COLLIER

Well, we're back with day two now. And, it's time for us to talk about the areas deep inside of us that are affected by abuse. I know it's only day two but it's time for us to see what's underneath our pain. To see the real wounds that abuse causes and all of the things that it steals from us. So strap in, cover yourself in prayer, and let's go get that healing and hope we all so desperately need.

14 "If you'll hold on to me for dear life," says God, "I'll get you out of any trouble. I'll give you the best of care if you'll only get to know and trust me. 15 Call me and I'll answer, be at your side in bad times; I'll rescue you, then throw you a party.

PSALM 91:14-15 (MSG)

1 You who sit down in the High God's presence, spend the night in Shaddai's shadow, 2 Say this: "God, you're my refuge. I trust in you and I'm safe!" 3 That's right—he rescues you from hidden traps, shields you from deadly hazards. 4 His huge outstretched arms protect you—under them you're perfectly safe; his arms fend off all harm. 5 Fear nothing—not wild wolves in the night, not flying arrows in the day, 6 Not disease that prowls through the darkness, not disaster that erupts at high noon. 7 Even though others succumb all around,

drop like flies right and left, no harm will even graze you. [8] You'll stand untouched, watch it all from a distance, watch the wicked turn into corpses. [9] Yes, because God's your refuge, the High God your very own home, [10] Evil can't get close to you, harm can't get through the door. [11] He ordered his angels to guard you wherever you go. [12] If you stumble, they'll catch you; their job is to keep you from falling. [13] You'll walk unharmed among lions and snakes, and kick young lions and serpents from the path. [14] "If you'll hold on to me for dear life," says God, "I'll get you out of any trouble. I'll give you the best of care if you'll only get to know and trust me. [15] Call me and I'll answer, be at your side in bad times; I'll rescue you, then throw you a party. [16] I'll give you a long life, give you a long drink of salvation!"

PSALM 91:14-15 (MSG)

One day my mom and I were shopping in Walmart. I had to have been in my late elementary school years because I was still playing in the racks of the clothes that my mom was shopping in. I remember when she wasn't looking I decided that I would hide in one of the circular racks right in the middle so she couldn't find me.

I waited. And waited. And then I got scared. I peaked my head out of the rack and my mom was nowhere to be found. My heart completely dropped and I don't know if it's because I've always been dramatic, but my mind immediately went to; "I'm not going to have parents. No one knows where I am. I'm not gonna have anyone to protect

me and love me and nurture me. My life is over."
And, right there in that moment, I heard a faint
voice yelling, "Nae! Nae! Where are you?!" It
was my mom, that same sheer panic that I felt
in that moment she felt the moment she didn't
have eyes on me. She was afraid that she wouldn't
have a daughter; she didn't know where I was, and
she was afraid that her life as a parent to her only
daughter would be over.

Abuse has a way of making us feel like we're in a
circular rack. All alone, trapped, without rescue,
and right here in those trapped and fearful places
we can lose our identity very easily. The voice of
God that we may have so easily recognized before
becomes that very distant voice that's almost

unrecognizable. And isn't that just what the enemy
wants? Isn't that the place he had Eve when he lured
her into the garden, all alone, distant from the voice
of God, filling her head with lies and confusion.
And it's there in that place that we begin to believe
the lies of the enemy; alone, forgotten about, dumb,
naïve, and too far gone.

Well, here's the good news. When David writes his
beautiful poem in Psalm 91, he reminds us of just
how fatherly our God is and just how much He's
reaching after us, calling our name across the isles
of darkness and fear that are in between us and

him. When I followed my mom's voice, when I stop for a moment to just calm myself and just listen to her voice, she found me. What would it look like for you to calm your mind, detach from the distractions, recognize the lies the enemy is trying to sell and trade them out for the truth that there is a guy chasing after you and wants nothing more than to find, rescue, and throw you a party?

PRAYER FOR TODAY

Let's pray. God, there are moments when I am afraid, alone and lost. In those moments, right there in those places of sheer panic, would you remind me that I can reach out to you for help in rescue? Would you create in my heart a pathway to pursue bravery and escape and ultimately trusting you? God, protect me as I make the hard decisions to get out of hiding and walk bodly in the truth that I am your daughter and I am worth saving. In Jesus' name, amen.

_3_

BREAK EVERY CYCLE

TONI COLLIER

———————————

Well, you made it to day three, and that's a big deal. Can we just stop for a moment and congratulate you? Wherever you're reading, give yourself a pat on the back and maybe a quick, "You go girl!" in the mirror. Whatever you do, my hope is that you know that you're doing great and holy and hard work. Keep going, today we're talking about breaking cycles. This is where the real work and ultimately the seeds of change can be birthed and harvested.

> *For our struggle is not against flesh and blood, but against the rulers,*
> *against the authorities, against the powers of this dark world*
> *and against the spiritual forces of evil in the heavenly realms.*

EPHESIANS 6:12 (ESV)

[10] Finally, be strong in the Lord and in his mighty power. [11] Put on the full armor of God, so that you can take your stand against the devil's schemes. [12] For our struggle is not against flesh and blood, but against the rulers, against the authorities, against the powers of this dark world and against the spiritual forces of evil in the heavenly realms. [13] Therefore put on the full armor of God, so that when the day of evil comes, you may be able to stand your ground,

and after you have done everything, to stand. ¹⁴ Stand firm then, with the belt of truth buckled around your waist, with the breastplate of righteousness in place, ¹⁵ and with your feet fitted with the readiness that comes from the gospel of peace. ¹⁶ In addition to all this, take up the shield of faith, with which you can extinguish all the flaming arrows of the evil one. ¹⁷ Take the helmet of salvation and the sword of the Spirit, which is the word of God. ¹⁸ And pray in the Spirit on all occasions with all kinds of prayers and requests. With this in mind, be alert and always keep on praying for all the Lord's people. ¹⁹ Pray also for me, that whenever I speak, words may be given me so that I will fearlessly make known the mystery of the gospel, ²⁰ for which I am an ambassador in chains. Pray that I may declare it fearlessly, as I should.

EPHESIANS 6:10-20 (ESV)

When I look at my story, I see so many cycles of abuse. From when I was a little girl and my cousins taking advantage of me sexually, to my dad being verbally abusive calling me names that I pray one day leave my memory, to an abusive marriage and a spiritually abusive church experience. Abuse is real in all parts of my story and in almost every season leading up to 25. But it was there, at my 25th birthday, that I made a decision that the cycles of abuse would no longer be a part of my story. I made a decision that along with God I could rewrite my story, I could heal from the wounds that had taken over my identity, and I could pave a new way for my daughter, for my friends, my

about trying not to bite your nails or drinking way too much coffee and overspending when anxiety comes. Breaking the cycle of abuse in your life is about recognizing where the enemy has taken ground in spiritually misaligned parts of your life that need real healing in the same power that raised Jesus from the dead. In Ephesians chapter 6, we find what it takes to defeat these types of cycles. In the first step is to recognize that the struggle is not against flesh and blood, but it is against the powers of this dark world, if we are going to fight, then it won't require intellect and it won't require fists—it will demand our kneeling.

community and the people and women and I get to minister to. I was just done with abuse; whether it be at the hand of the people I allowed in my life and chose or from the people that forced their way in, there was a cycle, a clear repetition of abuse, and it was time that I break it.

When we go to God and ask for protection from the enemy, we begin to speak directly to our unseen enemy about the deeply rooted cycles that he's planted or is trying to plant in our lives; that's when we ultimately begin to unravel and rewrite our stories. Is this your 25th birthday moment? Are you ready to begin a journey of breaking every dark force that has come to stand in your way? Read Ephesians 6, get your armor ready, girl, and let's go win the battle back.

What I learned about these types of cycles that need to be broken is that they aren't your everyday bad habit. This isn't about eating chocolate chip cookies every night (which I do a lot), this isn't

PRAYER FOR TODAY

Let's pray for the breaking of abusive cycles. Lord, I know that I have an unseen enemy, and I know that he wants nothing more than my feminine beautiful heart to be destroyed. God, open my eyes to the schemes of the enemy, then remind me of the tools that I have available in your Word and your spirit that can help me win the battle for the life that you have promised. And lastly, Lord, would you be with me through it all? Would you hold my hand? Will you walk with me? Will you guide my feet? Standing on your promises, in Jesus' name, amen.

4

SHAKE IT OFF

TONI COLLIER

Wow, you're doing great. Day four is here, and it's time for us to shake some things off of our hearts. Oftentimes when we go through reviews, we are left in a cycle of shame. We're embarrassed, we're ashamed of the choices that we made, we feel like it's all our fault, and that's right where the enemy wants us. He wants us to feel so ashamed of what we've been through that we force ourselves not to feel it. And the truth is if we don't feel it, we can't heal it. So let's go shake some things off, girl.

The Lord is merciful and gracious, slow to anger and abounding in steadfast love.

PSALM 103:8-12 (ESV)

The Lord is merciful and gracious, slow to anger and abounding in steadfast love. He will not always chide, nor will he keep his anger forever. He does not deal with us according to our sins, nor repay us according to our iniquities. For as high as the heavens are above the earth, so great is his steadfast love toward those who fear him; as far as the east is from the west, so far does he remove our transgressions from us.

PSALM 103:8-12 (ESV)

You've heard it before, social media is a highlight reel. But have you ever thought about why it's become that? Have you ever thought about why people choose to post only the best parts of their lives? I'd say about 40% of people are using social media as a way to make money, be profitable and so their content has to look and feel a certain way. But, the vast majority of people only post beautiful, perfect things because we enjoy the attention. We enjoy the likes and the comments and the follows. And, we're afraid that if people really knew how many times we yelled at our kids, how many times he slipped back into that addiction, how much we battle with anxiety and trusting new people in our lives, that maybe they wouldn't give us as much attention as we want and so desperately need. So, we take all the broken pieces of our lives and we lock them away with the keys of shame, and then you take all the pretty parts and put them on display when all the while our souls are yearning for a deep connection, to be seen and known and accepted flaws and all.

So what do we do with all that shame? How do we get to places where we accept that as humans we are imperfect and guilty but that we don't have to live in shame? We can proclaim that our stories, our pain, and our darkness don't have to be locked up in a vault. We can share all the broken parts of ourselves and still bask in the wondrous glory of our father.

Here's how:

1. Clearly differentiate guilt and shame. We are all guilty, we all fall short, but shame binds us to pre-resurrection mentality. Guilt says, "I've done something bad," but shame says, "I am bad." Shame is an identity stealer and an attack from the enemy that you don't have to give in to. Accept that you may not get things

right, deny that you can't be redeemed and made new again every day.

2. Trade the lies of the enemy with truth from the Father. Shame is fed by isolation and doubt; it's destroyed, however, by compassion and biblical truth. Spend time with God asking Him to infuse His truth into your heart.

3. Find healthy, whole and holy community. We need this to thrive. We need to be seen at our lowest and told that we matter by people who can carry it. Ask God to send you people who can keep you out of shame cycles and hiding and build you up.

Friend, it's time for us to shake shame off and out of our lives and believe that "The Lord is merciful and gracious, slow to anger and abounding in steadfast love" (Psalm 103:8 NIV.) There's nothing to be ashamed of. He knows our pasts, and His love is still so steadfast.

PRAYER FOR TODAY

Let's pray this together. I am your daughter, Lord, and there's nothing that I've done or that has happened to me that can take your love away. You created me to be free and living an unembarrassed life. That is the Eden you wanted for me. And while I know sin tried to destroy that freedom for me, I also know that you sent your son to give me a fair chance at living in that freedom. God, don't let the enemy convince me that I should hide , and help me to live a bold, unashamed life. In Jesus' name, amen.

5

EYE ON THE PRIZE

TONI COLLIER

It's day five and you have been on a journey of pursuing healing and wholeness. You've done the hard work of recognizing and accepting that you are worthy of freedom and safety and God's grace. You've begun to realize that God is pursuing and chasing after you and He wants you to get on the other side of this dark season because He wants to throw you a party and celebrate His incredible daughter. You've hopefully started to identify the dark cycles that have been perpetuated and continued in your life and now you're proclaiming freedom from those cycles. Today is all about the focus that's needed to not only walk in new-found freedom and acceptance of who you are but to hold your head high while doing it. So, let's talk about how you do that.

> *25 Keep your head up, your eyes straight ahead, and your focus fixed on what is in front of you. 26 Take care you don't stray from the straight path, the way of truth, and you will safely reach the end of your road. 27 Do not veer off course to the right or the left; step away from evil, and leave it behind.*

PROVERBS 4:25-27 (VOICE)

My husband, Sam, tells the story when he talks to future leaders or those that are looking to find purpose and be successful. He describes a time when he had a mentor of his who he had gone to complaining that nothing in his life was working out, that there was no way out of the dark hole that he was in and he needed help. His mentor put them in a room that had glass doors, set a bottle on a chair and across from that bottle he had Sam sit down and he instructed him to look at that bottle, stare at it until he came back. 10 minutes went by, 30 minutes, an hour. His mentor came back and Sam asked him, "Why are you making me do this?" He said, "Don't worry about it; I'll explain later. Keep looking at the bottle, and I'll be back." Another hour passed by, and Sam was so confused. His mentor came back and said, "The greatest threat to your success, to truly getting to the other side of hope and purpose in your life, is your inability to focus."

Oftentimes, the enemy, who is the ultimate distractor, will take us off of a beautiful path of healing and hope and wholeness and distract us with triggers and reminders of our past. It does take a while for our brain to heal and for us to be able to carry scars and not wounds; there is also a level of looking back that will rob us of our future ability to walk in freedom. You deserve to walk in freedom. You deserve to be able to look at the future of your life and realize that there is hope. That abuse can no longer define you, keep you captive, and rob you of what's available for your beautiful heart. But, we have to learn how to focus. We have to learn how to be intentional about the journey that God has reset our lives on. We have to learn how to keep our eye on the prize.

King Solomon in Proverbs 4:25-27 (VOICE), says so eloquently, "Keep your head up, your eyes straight ahead, and your focus fixed on what is in front of you. Take care you don't stray from the straight path, the way of truth, and you will safely reach the end of your road. Do not veer off course to the right or the left; step away from evil, and leave it behind." God has you on a beautiful path of truth; it's why

you're doing this study. Because you want freedom and you want truth and safety and you wanna leave behind the things that have hurt you and left you hurt.

So, keep your head up, and keep your eye on the prize. On the other side of your focus on Jesus is a beautiful reminder that abuse doesn't get the final say.

PRAYER FOR TODAY

Let's pray. Thank you, father. Thank you for meeting me here on this journey. Thank you for reminding me that I have Worth that can't be taken, that you're continually chasing after me, and that you want the best for me. God, when it gets hard, when the enemy tries to steal my focus, would you just be with me and help me remain focused on where you want me to go? Would you remind me that my North Star is always Jesus. I love you, and it's in your son Jesus' name I pray, amen.

Summary

Defeating Abuse/Abusive Cycles

Overcoming that "trapped" and "labeled" feeling

Worth: Your worth isn't tied to how you have been treated

There is still hope to be fought for and reached for.

There is no darkness Jesus can't touch, and there is no pain we can't come back from. We cannot be defeated. We are overcomers.

6

REAL LOVE

SEWA FIELDS

Hi friend, it's Sewa. Let's talk about LOVE. Yes, LOVE. When we know what real love looks like, we can see the cycle of abuse more clearly. Join me won't you? Let God's unending love be the place where you know who and whose you are.

"Love is patient, love is kind. It does not envy, it does not boast, it is not proud. It does not dishonor others, it is not self-seeking, it is not easily angered, it keeps no record of wrongs. Love does not delight in evil but rejoices with the truth. It always protects, always trusts, always hopes, always perseveres. Love never fails..."

1 CORINTHIANS 13:4-8 (NIV)

Let's start with LOVE. This is a good place; this is the foundation by which we must grow and rise from the pain of abuse. Maybe you're reading these words and realizing that you have never been loved in a pure and beautiful way. Love has been defiled by the hurtful words, manipulation and physical wounds of your abuser. You may never be able to understand real love if you measured it against the actions and words of those who you trusted the most. Love has been distorted and used against you. You may be left wondering: What does real love really look like?

Real Love, dear friend, seeks the benefit of the other. Real love speaks words of life and affirmation when no one else is listening. Real love takes a moment to breathe instead of acting in anger. Real love chooses sincerity rather than a false public display of affection. Real love sacrifices one's selfish ambition. Real love's name is Jesus.

He who laid down His life for you to gain nothing for Himself. He who left the glory of heaven to become a mere man on your behalf. He made himself man so that He could understand your pain and know your weakness so that He could grieve when you are grieving. Jesus is a kind, caring, patient protector whose love for you knows no bounds. He is your example of real and undefiled love. Learn from Him, lean into Him and live your life with the knowledge that you are deeply loved by the God of the universe.

This is our measure of real love, and it's so very good and perfect.

"For as high as the heavens are above the earth, so great is his steadfast love."

PSALM 103:11 (ESV)

PRAYER FOR TODAY

Father, thank you for your unfathomable love for each of us. Father, give us eyes to see the depths of your love for us despite the imperfections of human love. Father, give us the courage to rest in your caring hands when life has tried to break us. Father, thank you for the model you have set before us. I pray that we may understand your love for us in the depths of our soul and that we may live it out in our love for others. In Jesus' name, amen.

7

SPEAK YOUR TRUTH

SEWA FIELDS

Disclaimer: today might be a difficult step because today we are talking about speaking up, voicing your truth and letting your story be heard. The world needs your story. We all do.

For God has not given us a spirit of fear, but of power and of love and of a sound mind.

2 TIMOTHY 1:7 (NKJV)

If you've been in an abusive relationship, you know that secrecy is the unsaid expectation that looms over you. In fact, abuse thrives in the secret places; it grows in the shadows, and the more it is kept in hiding, the harder it is to bring it to the light. The lines of reality become blurred, and eventually you are living a duplicitous life between the pain on the inside and the "happy" life that's showing on the outside. The pressure to maintain this dynamic along with the fear of leaving and other people's opinions can easily make us feel trapped in a cycle that feels impossible to overcome.

Friend, no matter how mucky and difficult it is, speaking the truth to yourself and others will set you free. The truth has a way of doing that. When we shine a light on the darkness in our lives, it gives us clarity that only the light can bring. There is a

relief in using your words and speaking your pain out loud. Your words and your story have power to bring healing and restoration to that which has been broken within you.

Let it be known that speaking your truth is an incredibly bold and courageous step. I believe we, as women, already know the consequences we may face for shining a light on the abuse that has been done to us. We have already seen many women who have paid the price for speaking the truth, and we know that that may become our reality as well.

Dear sister, God sees the tension and angst that you have faced. He knows the price you have had to pay to stay and the price you will pay to leave. He knows the fears that accompany these decisions, but He also knows the life of freedom that you can have ahead of you.

God's heart for you is to live an authentic life with confidence and peace of mind. Let's hold on to the truth in this verse for young Timothy as he faced many fears and trials of his own. "For God has not given us a spirit of fear, but of power and of love and of a sound mind." (2 Timothy 1:7, NKJV). Paul reminds Timothy that while it's normal to have fear, we cannot let fear overwhelm us. That as we walk in truth, He will give us perfect peace even in the midst of great trials. Isaiah 26:3 states "You will keep in perfect peace all who trust in you, all whose thoughts are fixed on you!"

God, in His mercy, exchanges our fear with a spirit of power, love and a sound mind. What a beautiful promise we can hold on to. God is with us, He is for us and when He is on our side, nothing can come against us. We have nothing to fear; we can make bold moves with God's strength.

PRAYER FOR TODAY

Father, we come before you as frail humans that are in need of your strength. We know that in our own strength we are afraid and not able to speak up. Father, we claim today a spirit of power and sound mind that you desire to give us. We pray that you may empower us with boldness and courage to speak our stories. We pray that you will use these stories for our restoration and healing. We pray that these stories will bring glory to your name in every way. In Jesus' name I pray, amen.

8

YOU ARE DEFINED BY YOUR CREATOR

SEWA FIELDS

Yesterday was a big one. Now, today, join me as we dig in to what our Father says about who we are in Him. Do you know how precious you are? Do you know that your value isn't based on your circumstances? Do you know your place in the Kingdom?

"³ *All praise to God, the Father of our Lord Jesus Christ, who has blessed us with every spiritual blessing in the heavenly realms because we are united with Christ.* ⁴ *Even before he made the world, God loved us and chose us in Christ to be holy and without fault in his eyes.* ⁵ *God decided in advance to adopt us into his own family by bringing us to himself through Jesus Christ. This is what he wanted to do, and it gave him great pleasure.* ⁶ *So we praise God for the glorious grace he has poured out on us who belong to his dear Son.* ⁷ *He is so rich in kindness and grace that he purchased our freedom with the blood of his Son and forgave our sins.* ⁸ *He has showered his kindness on us, along with all wisdom and understanding.*

⁹ *God has now revealed to us his mysterious will regarding Christ—which is to fulfill his own good plan.* ¹⁰ *And this is the plan: At the right time he will bring everything together under the authority of Christ—everything in heaven and on earth.*"

EPHESIANS 1:3-10

My dear sister, people may look upon you by your circumstance. They may see what was done to you rather than WHO you are. They may know you by these words: abused, defiled, used. The world sees a shattered woman, but God sees a created being that has always been beautiful and whole. You are the light of His life. Your circumstance has never changed your glory. Who you were in your mother's womb, precious and loved, is who you are now.

Our troubles will make us forget the truths of God's Word. Our trials can easily make us, doubt the value that we hold. No matter the words that were spoken over your heart, you are a treasure worth loving.

In Ephesians Chapter 1, the apostle Paul is writing to the church in Ephesus reminding them of their new identity in Christ. His words are profound and a proclamation of truth over the false beliefs that we sometimes hold.

Let's claim these words for ourselves today, gals:

1. We have been chosen and called for a greater purpose than our pain.

2. God has lavished every spiritual blessing upon us, and we are the heirs of His Kingdom.

3. We have been adopted into God's family, not cast aside or abandoned.

4. We have been redeemed, called blameless and forgiven.

5. We have the hope of eternity, and one day all things will be made new.

6. Our identity will never be altered by what has happened to us or by what we have done but by who we are in Christ alone.

Beloved, when God calls your name, all else pales in the light of His blessing over your life.

Go live confidently in who you are and whose you are.

PRAYER FOR TODAY

Father, we are so thankful that we are not rejected but we are accepted and chosen by you. Our circumstances will not define us, but they will mold us closer to your image. Thank you for inviting us to share in your inheritance. We are undeserving, but you are faithful to give us more than what we deserve. Father, help these truths to sink in deep and make their place in our spirits so that we can live them out for your glory. In Jesus' name, amen.

9

NEVER DEFEATED

SEWA FIELDS

Ever heard the phrase "When it rains it pours"? Life can feel like this sometimes, when we face too many devastating challenges at the same time. Thankfully, God's Word tells us that though we are overwhelmed on all sides, we will not despair or be defeated!! WOOH! Join me as we hold on to this promise!

> *8 We are pressed on every side by troubles, but we are not crushed. We are perplexed, but not driven to despair. 9 We are hunted down, but never abandoned by God. We get knocked down, but we are not destroyed.*

2 CORINTHIANS 4:8-9

In life, we are constantly living at the intersection of hurt and hope. Broken but hopeful. We can hold the suffering of the current life and the promises of a better future in the same hand. We can hold pain and see the beauty in it in the same breath. "Hurt and Hope can coexist." (Jenna Carver)

In this scripture passage, this message is so clearly pronounced. Although you may be in a season of crushing, it will not destroy you. God has never abandoned you. He has never forsaken you, and although you may feel overwhelmed, you can still claim His beautiful promises over your life.

He has always had a way out for you. Our circumstances may push us to the brink of despair, but God will never allow us to be completely consumed. He will not let us be defeated. He is the God of Abraham who has remained faithful from the beginning of time. His promises over your life will never be deterred.

"Let us hold tightly without wavering to the hope we affirm, for God can be trusted to keep his promise."

HEBREWS 10:23

The translation of these verses in 2 Corinthians 4:8-9 by William Barclay is beautiful and poignant here:

"We are sore pressed at every point, but not hemmed in; we are at our wit's end, but never at our hope's end; we are persecuted by men, but never abandoned by God; we are knocked down, but not knocked out."

Say these truths with me, dear sister:

1. I am not defeated by my insecurities; I stand in confidence in Christ alone.

2. I am not defeated by my pain, God has a purpose in this, even still.

3. I am not defeated by my feelings of rage; I have the capacity to forgive.

4. I am not defeated by my fears; I can have a sound mind through Christ Jesus.

5. I am not defeated by my wounds; I can be healed in Jesus' name.

6. I am not defeated, I am an overcomer; a conqueror in Christ Jesus.

Beloved, "it may be necessary to encounter the defeats, so you can know who you are, what you can rise from and how you can still come out of it."

MAYA ANGELOU

PRAYER FOR TODAY

Father, we come before you today with so much gratitude that you came to Earth for us, you gave your life for us, you defeated sin and death so that we can live this beautiful, abundant life. We can face our own defeats because we have a God who has faced defeat on our behalf. We praise you for the mercy you give us in our moments of despair. We praise you for the capacity to heal for the wounds that try to bind us. We praise you that you are a God that gives us the grace to hold hope while we heal. We love you, Jesus. In Jesus' name I pray, amen.

10

YOUR PURPOSE IS GREATER THAN YOUR PAIN

SEWA FIELDS

Today we look forward to all that God has ahead for us. We look forward
in hope, for we know our God is faithful to redeem every loss and hurt!

"See I am doing a new thing! Now it springs up; Do you not perceive it?
I am making a way in the wilderness and streams in the desert."

ISAIAH 43:19 (NIV)

When I walked through the devastation of an abusive relationship and a subsequent divorce, I struggled tremendously to find meaning within the pain and loss. They say that the depth of your grief is equivalent to the measure you loved that person. The loss of trust, loss of relationship, loss of everything that I knew to be true was more than I could bear at times. I kept telling myself that there must be a reason behind this pain, but all I wanted was a different story that didn't involve this tragedy.

I struggled to hold on to hope as all I could see before me were ashes; the remains of dreams I held of a beautiful life, were now all gone.

But God....

God looked over this landscape of devastating loss and began to breathe hope into the small crevices of my heart that needed His life. He began to shine His light through the broken cracks, slowly but surely reminding my soul of these beautiful truths. Even here, even when there is nothing to hold on to, He will make a way. He will mend my broken heart and bring me to a place of wholeness.

He will do the impossible because that's His speciality.

Beloved, God doesn't break us unless He has something greater to accomplish through that suffering.

What the enemy meant for evil in your life, God has destined for a greater good. He will use your story for a purpose bigger than you will ever imagine. Even as I am writing these words to you, I am reminded how God is using my story to bring meaning to my pain and yours.

In your deepest suffering, you will learn the deepest lessons about the love of the Father for you. Out of your grief, you will have the unshakable mark of His presence over your life, and these lessons will never leave you. This season will always be a defining moment in your life of how the Father rescued you and gave you new life.

C.S. Lewis (who was no stranger to grief) noted that "God whispers in our pleasures and shouts in our pain. It is His megaphone to rouse a deaf world." He will take what would have left you devastated and use it to move you closer to Him and make you more like Him. He will take the lessons you learned to heal someone else in the same place of pain.

He is the God who redeems. All of it. Nothing goes to waste.

You will be able to offer hope because once upon a time, you needed it, too! Don't look back; look ahead with hope.

He is doing a new thing, and it is beautiful!

PRAYER FOR TODAY

Father, only you can make a way where there is absolutely no other way. Only you have the power to take the utterly broken and mend it into something even more beautiful. We are in awe of your goodness, your faithfulness and the redemptive power of your hands. We bring these wounds before you and ask that you take them and use them as you see fit, for our good and for your glory. In all these things, we will be grateful for your hands that give blessings and allow pain, because you build a purpose out of everything. We praise you, Father in Heaven, because you are so worthy! In Jesus' name, amen.

Summary

Defeating Anxiety.

Healing from anxiety/anxious cycles is not an "arrival" or an "x-marks-the-spot"; it can be an everyday challenge with some seasons feeling heavier than others.

Encouragement/Reminders for clawing your way out of anxious moments/seasons.

There is no darkness Jesus can't touch, and there is no pain we can't come back from. We cannot be defeated. We are overcomers.

11

IDENTIFYING AND UPROOTING

HOPE MOQUIN

Hey sis, it's Hope. And man... Anxiety is a sneaky weight that creeps in on you out of nowhere at times. Knowing where it stems from will help you know where to speak to it.

"For I do not understand my own actions. For I do not do what I want, but I do the very thing I hate. Now if I do what I do not want, I agree with the law, that it is good. So now it is no longer I who do it, but sin that dwells within me. For I know that nothing good dwells in me, that is, in my flesh. For I have the desire to do what is right, but not the ability to carry it out. For I do not do the good I want, but the evil I do not want is what I keep on doing. Now if I do what I do not want, it is no longer I who do it, but sin that dwells within me."

ROMANS 7:15-20 (ESV)

Many of us get frustrated with ourselves in how we react and how we behave, but we haven't asked the Lord to show us where it all began. So many of us don't understand why we do some of the things we don't want to do. Why certain responses set something off inside our souls. Why some words that seem so small hurt so deeply. Why we run towards things that we know aren't good for us. You know who understood this? Paul.

Talk about relatability. There are many habits you and I carry which we don't necessarily like. There are ways you and I react in which we know are not holy. There are mindsets you and I have which we know are not beneficial for us. Which is one of the reasons why there is such a need for God and His grace in humanity. There is a God who is bold and who is big. A God who is sitting on the edge of His seat waiting for us to open our hands and simply say, "I need you, God." That is His joy. Helping our frail human hearts and eyes see our roots. All for the purpose of allowing our human hearts to know Him a little bit more.

What's your root? Maybe it's the way your mom or dad wasn't there for you the way you wanted them to be. Maybe it's from a family member, or friend. Maybe it's from a pastor. Ouch. That's a really real one, too. The thing about roots is they are often formed from experiences that were out of our control. There was not any way to prevent the way that someone rejected us, and there was not anything we could do about the actions of others. We cannot prevent the actions of others, but we can control our responses. Though the way the root was created is out of our control, the way we go back and shed light on the root is our choice.

I don't know what your root may be, but ask the Lord to show you. One thing that I have learned is that the Lord will not ever reveal something that He does not intend to heal. What it was, does not always have to be. Be bold. Ask God with an expectancy to show you.

PRAYER FOR TODAY

Pray with me.

Lord, I pray you open my eyes to see you in all things. I pray you give me clarity and wisdom to see the roots in my life and that you would shed light on them. I trust you, Lord, with all of my heart, and I lean not on my own understanding, but in all my ways I acknowledge you. I trust that your plan for my life is good, and I will rest in this. Amen.

12

REMEMBER WHOSE YOU ARE

HOPE MOQUIN

It was when Hagar remembered where she came from, and why she started, that she was able to obtain the promise that the Lord had for her. She was able to stomp on the fears and the anxiety when she was able to rest who she was in the Father's eyes.

> *The angel of the Lord found Hagar beside a spring of water in the wilderness, along the road to Shur. The angel said to her, "Hagar, Sarai's servant, where have you come from, and where are you going?" "I'm running away from my mistress, Sarai," she replied.*
>
> *The angel of the Lord said to her, "Return to your mistress, and submit to her authority." Then he added, "I will give you more descendants than you can count."*
>
> *And the angel also said, "You are now pregnant and will give birth to a son. You are to name him Ishmael (which means 'God hears'), for the Lord has heard your cry of distress. This son of yours will be a wild man, as untamed as a wild donkey! He will raise his fist against everyone, and everyone will be against him. Yes, he will live in open hostility against all his relatives.*
>
> *Thereafter, Hagar used another name to refer to the Lord, who had spoken to her. She said, "You are the God who sees me." She also said, "Have I truly seen the One who sees me?"*

GENESIS 16:7-13

It is not difficult to make decisions when you know what you value. It's evident that Hagar was so moved by the voice of God that she chose to go back, therefore proving she valued what God had for her. Here's the thing. If it takes your attention, it's not worth it. This can be people, relationships, friendships, addictions, habits, and even thought patterns.

What can we classify as evil? Anything that would take our attention off of Him. "Turn away" in the original text literally means to turn off. Meaning to refuse acceptance to, to send away, to reject. So what this is saying... is to reject anything that may take our attention off of Him, even if it be for a moment.

And this will be the core and the backbone in our influence.

Hagar made a choice that though her emotions were shouting at her, "it's not worth it to stay," she had the ability to shut it down. And only she had that ability. In my experiences, I have learned that nobody can determine what our values are except for us. Everyone can speak into what they think should be important to us, and everybody loves trying to decide what the right path is for us. But when it comes down to it, we are the only ones who have the honor of choosing what is going to hold value in our lives.

It's easy to let our circumstances shape our beliefs and even hinder what we thought was important to us. It's inevitable that at times, we may disengage ourselves with our core values. We may shift our beliefs to fill the empty spaces we encounter, and we may even drop our beliefs based on the pain we have experienced from carrying them in the first place. I believe that is what Hagar

encountered. She knew what was important to her, but her circumstance was so heavy it was shoving her values beneath her. But she made a choice to rise up against her flesh and listen to what the Lord was saying. Even when it didn't make sense. To call upon God and let Him strengthen her when anxiety and stress was trying to keep her down.

PRAYER FOR TODAY

Pray with me. Lord, I pray you bring me to remembrance in knowing who you have made me to be. I ask and declare for godly confidence found in you for when I am weak. Open my ears to hear your words over my own thoughts. I pray that you build me up in your love and that my heart will fall more in love with you today. I pray that I will stand on and trust in the uncompromised Word of God. Amen.

13

ENOUGH IS ENOUGH

HOPE MOQUIN

When Jesus came down from the mountainside, large crowds followed him. A man with leprosy came and knelt before him and said, "Lord, if you are willing, you can make me clean."

MATTHEW 8:1-2 (NIV)

I think we all inadvertently accept less than what we stand for sometimes. Maybe because we get frustrated, or maybe because we think what we stand for is too much at times.

It's not easy, but we need to learn how to get tired of tolerating conditions that are not in line with our surety. It's not popular, but we need to learn how to get tired of saying yes to things that our hearts are shouting no. It's not effortless, but we need to learn how to get tired of trying on people's opinions as if those are what we are going to wear when everything is all said and done. You see, settling is more than just accepting less than. Settling is choosing comfort over calling. And I have never known someone worth looking up to because of their comfortability and commitment to average. But it's the people who learned how to get tired of certain habits, certain friendships, certain relationships (come on somebody), and certain

ways of thinking — those people. The people who are silently different simply because of their spiritual fight.

The thing about the leper is he was walking around with something he was cursed with that was out of his control. There was not a single thing he could have done on his own to get rid of his condition. Like many of us, there are things that were passed down to us that we couldn't stop. There were things that have happened to us that we couldn't stop. There are habits that we carry that we cannot get rid of. There are mindsets that consume us that we can't change. But here's the thing about Jesus. There are legalistic people who have complained that Jesus violated the law in this story. For it was completely

unlawful to touch a leper. And there goes Jesus. Doing His thing.

So, this man, the leper, had a condition that he could no longer feel because it progressed so rapidly. He had a condition that was essentially killing him day by day, and there was no human touch that could relieve him of this tragedy. But what I admire is the Leper came to Jesus by himself despite how many discouragements he would encounter.

"Lord, if You are willing"

The leper had no doubt whatsoever about the ability of Jesus to heal. He was bold. His only question was if Jesus was willing to heal. It won't always make sense. Sometimes, it's going to be real hard. But I believe if we allow ourselves to give way even a tiny bit to what God is trying to do then, I believe and rest in the holy truth that we're in good hands. He's well worth trusting. You are an influencer. And I beg for you to walk that out. No more pasts, no more insecurities, and no more doubts. Go all in. The Lord has too much planned for you to sit back and contemplate the day you want to speak up.

PRAYER FOR TODAY

Lord, I pray you calm my heart today. I pray you give me the boldness to approach you and the faith to believe that you will do it. I pray for peace and comfort. I pray that you instill in me a faith that will not be compromised and that you will keep my foot from being caught. I trust you, God. Amen

14

FINDING GOOD IN THE PLACES THAT SHOUT BAD

HOPE MOQUIN

"Every time you cross my mind, I break out in exclamations of thanks to God. Each exclamation is a trigger to prayer. I find myself praying for you with a glad heart. I am so pleased that you have continued on in this with us, believing and proclaiming God's Message, from the day you heard it right up to the present. There has never been the slightest doubt in my mind that the God who started this great work in you would keep at it and bring it to a flourishing finish on the very day Christ Jesus appears."

PHILIPPIANS 1:3-6
THE MESSAGE (MSG)

I don't know you. I don't know what your upbringing looked like. I don't know what your life looks like right now. I don't know how many times you've fallen flat on your face over the same struggle. I don't know how many times you have considered calling quits. I don't know how deeply you've ached. But I do know how I have. I have

ached, and I still ache sometimes. We're human. I know mine and you know yours.

But we both can know a God who calls us friend. I don't know where you're at or where you've been, but we both can know a God who's with us even when everything is blurry. We both can know a

God who has orchestrated every detail for our life for something GOOD. We both can know a God who has seen us run away but who already knew where we would end up. We both can know a God who gives out chance after chance. We both can know a God is already on the floor ready to meet us before we even get there. We both can know a God who calms us in our frustration. We both can know a God who sees us. Who knows us. And who chooses us. Even when we can't see ourselves. Even when we don't know ourselves. Even when we would never choose ourselves. We both can know the God who picks us, every time. With no hesitation. Here's what I learned.

Good does not always shout good.
Good does not always fit comfortably.
Good is often hidden in really bad.
Good is not always an instant product
that is tangible.
Good is not always aligned with my feelings.
Good is not a subcomponent of faultless.

In fact, I found the greatest good in the
greatest mess.
In the middle of all the clutter, there was good.
In all of the restructuring, there was good.
In all of the opposite directions, there was good.
In all of the trips, there was good.

Good is not always loud and good is not always bright. On some days good is silent, and on some days good is cloudy. And here's the contradiction — those are the kind of days that I look back to and see the greatest gifts in. How clever is God to hide good in all the places that shout bad.

PRAYER FOR TODAY

God, I thank you for being present in every season. I thank you that I can trust you and that you are good. I pray you open my eyes to see you and experience your goodness. I pray your goodness overrides the doubt in my life and that you place a song in my heart for me to sing. I love you, God, and I trust you. Amen.

15

WHERE ELSE WOULD WE GO OTHER THAN TO JESUS?

HOPE MOQUIN

After this many of his disciples turned back and no longer walked with him. So Jesus said to the twelve, "Do you want to go away as well?" Simon Peter answered him, "Lord, to whom shall we go? You have the words of eternal life, and we have believed, and have come to know, that you are the Holy One of God."

JOHN 6:66-69 (ESV)

It was one of Peter's sweetest proclamations—out of a passionate heart and of an authentic love. There was no one else who could show him the right way.

His response spoke, *"You are my God. On the mountain and in the valley. You were the God at the beginning and you are the God at the end. You are where every hungry soul finds a meal. Where every tired soul finds a place of rest. There isn't any other than you. In you there is grace and direction. In you there is security from every enemy. Who else is there other than you?"*

Simon Peter answered, *"You are the Messiah, the Son of the living God."*

MATTHEW 16:16 (NIV)

Was Peter perfect? Ha! No! But he had his eyes set unto what mattered to him. He had his heart in alignment with the heart of God. He got up when he fell down. He spent time with Jesus. Peter understood that the love of God is what frees us from sin not what frees us to sin. He spent time with Jesus to know the very heart of God, which is why he knew he could go back to the old relationships. He knew when anxiety crept in, he could go back to the self-doubt. He could go back to the normality of his life, to the parties, to the unhealthy habits. He could watch as EVERYONE was walking away. These people were probably his friends, and when it made sense to walk away with them, too, his response set the standard for Christianity today.

Peter knew the heart of God, so he chose to remain planted in what he knew was true. He didn't leave room to ponder. He didn't leave room to allow his mind and his own human logic to make a decision for him. When a life altering question was asked to Peter with every set of eyes watching him, he didn't have to go off and pray about what was the right choice. He was rooted in the truth of who Jesus was and who he was in Jesus. Therefore, when the question was asked, "Do you want to walk away, too?" He knew without a shadow of a doubt who Jesus was and where he stood.

And with weary hands and a heavy heart, I hope our heart repeats the same words he did. "Where else would I go?" In our weakest moments, I hope we still look at Jesus and with tear filled eyes choose to stand with Him knowing full well there is absolutely no place else we would rather be. I hope we run to Him before our fear runs into us. ▷▷▷

PRAYER FOR TODAY

God, I thank you for saving me. I thank you that you are good and that you are true. I pray my heart will find its home in you and that I will stand confidently on this. You are my rock and my salvation, and I will praise you all the days of my life. Amen.

Summary

Defeating Anxiety.

Healing from anxiety/anxious cycles is not an "arrival" or an "x-marks-the-spot"; it can be an everyday challenge with some seasons feeling heavier than others.

Encouragement/Reminders for clawing your way out of anxious moments/seasons.

There is no darkness Jesus can't touch, and there is no pain we can't come back from. We cannot be defeated. We are overcomers.

16

NAME IT AND SURRENDER IT TO GOD

NATHALIE MAXEY

Hi there! Nat, here. Over the next five days, we will be spending some time in Philippians 4:4-8 as we unpack how to overcome anxiety! I know that just by saying the word "anxiety" can make us feel anxious sometimes, but in order to get to the other side of it and live in peace and joy, we need to tackle it straightforwardly. So today's devo is all about that—getting to a point where we acknowledge our struggle with anxiety and take it before God in prayer.

> *Do not be anxious about anything, but in every situation, by prayer and petition, with thanksgiving, present your requests to God.*

PHILIPPIANS 4:6 (NIV)

I grew up in a very dysfunctional family and not really fitting into the mold of my Honduran culture. I rarely felt safe; instead, I often felt worried, paranoid, paralyzed, and even trapped. It was a very lonely and confusing world as this sense of doom hovered over me throughout my childhood and teen years. Even though the experience was traumatic by itself, the worst part was being in the dark about WHAT I was going through. It didn't matter how many times I was told, "be happy,"

"everything's fine," or "just relax and be free," nothing changed because it did not address the root issue! It wasn't until my mid-twenties when I finally realized that I had been dealing with anxiety, among other things, since a very young age!

If you're reading this and you can relate to these anxious, hopeless, and paralyzing feelings, please know that you're not alone! The journey of defeating anxiety begins right here, by simply recognizing that it is part of your brokenness. You've probably heard a variation of this saying: "you can't fix/heal what you don't know," and it's true! If you don't know what you're facing, like in my childhood, then you can't truly overcome it. It may not seem like much, but by calling it by name (hello anxiety), we can face it head on!

Now that you know that you're anxious (yay, welcome to the club)... what's next? While there are plenty of resources and therapy options that can be helpful, before you figure out treatment options, I encourage you to start by taking it to God in prayer. I know that anxiety is a very private matter for most of us, but you don't have to tackle it alone! I'm right here with you in this journey, and God wants to help you, too! He's simply waiting for you to be honest and transparent with Him. Verse 6 of Philippians 4 (NIV) says, "Do not be anxious about anything"—but it doesn't stop there; it's not a one-liner that dismisses your feelings or leaves you hanging. Instead, God wants to give you hope and show you HOW to "not be anxious!" Verse 6 continues to say, "in every situation, by prayer and petition, with thanksgiving, present your requests

to God." Whether it's the first or millionth time you recognize that anxiety is an issue in your life, present it before God believing that not only did He already know about it, but that He also has the answers to conquering this stronghold in your life. So, invite God to join you on this journey today, and ask Him to lead you to the other side of anxiety where His peace and joy are abundant!

PRAYER FOR TODAY

Dear Father, thank you for creating me so beautifully complex. Thank you for not making a mistake with me. You already know that anxiety is trying to claim a foothold over my life, but today I surrender my anxiety and mental health in your hands. You are my creator, my healer, and my savior. I ask you to guard my heart and my mind and to teach me how to overcome anxiety and live in your perfect peace.

In Jesus' name, amen.

17

CLING TO GOD'S SOVEREIGNTY
IN THIS WORLD'S UNCERTAINTY

NATHALIE MAXEY

Today, I want to let you in on one of the most pivotal and powerful truths regarding worry. In a world full of uncertainty and what if's, the only key to having true peace over anxiety comes by actively choosing God's sovereignty over our desire to control. It's not a magical step or item on a checklist (I wish it was!), but it's a lifelong habit that we have to nurture to break free from anxiety!

And the peace of God, which transcends all understanding,
will guard your hearts and your minds in Christ Jesus.

PHILIPPIANS 4:7 (NIV)

I am a planner. A lover of order and certainty. I like to know what's next (and what's after that). Why? Well, I grew up feeling like so much was happening out of my control; I felt powerless. So I learned to play it safe, avoid risks and anything that seemed uncertain, and to control anything I could. It was my make-shift way of finding security in a confusing world! What I didn't know, until recently, was that by over-controlling everything in my life, I was actually perpetuating the cycle of anxiety!

That's the truth, gal—anxiety thrives on uncertainty! When we focus on what we don't know and what-if

99

scenarios, our anxious thoughts run wild. They take our peace and even our sleep! You see, the key to overcoming anxiety in times of uncertainty is not in finding the "right" answer or even solving your problems. It lies in intentionally shifting your focus from what could or could not happen TO what is always true and certain. So what do we know to be constant? God's sovereignty and goodness, which have not changed through the ages! His all-knowing and all-powerful nature means that He's always in control. Nothing happens without Him knowing; even what surprises us (I see you, 2020), doesn't surprise God! Not only that, His kindness and faithfulness means that our lives are safe in His hands regardless of what we go through. What a relief!

I learned this lesson the hard way last year. 2020 was the year of the pandemic and social unrest,

but, for me, it was also the year when my body said, "enough!" I thought I was trusting God and was doing "fine," but the accumulated anxiety from the past few years, lack of sleep, and unhealthy habits caught up to me. I spent last year in "anxiety bootcamp" as chronic hives took over my whole life. Even though I was in excruciating pain and doctors couldn't find real answers, God gave me peace and showed me that He is kind and trustworthy. A year later, I'm doing much better, and I realize that if He can get me through last year, He can handle everything else in my life. That's how I know we can trust Him and continue letting go of my need for control! It's not because life is problem-free, but EVEN THOUGH I experienced some of the most difficult months in my adult life, God still used it for my good!

Philippians 4 verse 7 (NIV) says, "And the peace of God, which transcends all understanding, will guard your hearts and your minds in Christ Jesus." The peace that transcends all understanding, the peace that makes no sense based on our circumstances, is available on the other side of anxiety for you and for me! When you truly surrender your desire to know and control everything in your life, and decide to trust God with your actions (not just your words!), anxiety no longer has a stronghold over you!

PRAYER FOR TODAY

Dear Heavenly Father, there's no one like you. You are powerful and sovereign. You are so good and so kind. Today, I release my need to control my life and my future. I recognize that you are already on top of it. I trust you with everything I am and everything that I have because I know that you take care of me. No matter what comes my way, I choose to remember that you are with me and you are faithful. I choose to set my eyes on you and not my circumstances or fears. Increase my faith and fill my life with your peace that transcends all understanding and all circumstances. In Jesus' name, amen.

18

PREACH TO YOUR SOUL

NATHALIE MAXEY

Yesterday, we covered one of the most important truths about overcoming anxiety: while anxiety thrives on uncertainty, peace thrives on God's sovereignty and goodness. Today, I want to give you some practical steps on HOW you can practice doing just that!

> *Finally, brothers and sisters, whatever is true, whatever is noble, whatever is right, whatever is pure, whatever is lovely, whatever is admirable—if anything is excellent or praiseworthy—think about such things.*

PHILIPPIANS 4:8 (NIV)

We know that anxiety's ideal environment is filled with uncertainty, what if's obsessive thoughts, and our need for control. We also discovered the answer to breaking that anxious cycle—by shifting our attention to God's goodness and sovereignty. You may be thinking, "that sounds great in theory, but how do I live it out?"

While there's no magical or instant switch, here are some key things when facing an anxiety episode or stressful season. First, I encourage you to take deep breaths to calm your brain; I learned through my chronic illness that deep breathing truly helps our bodies and minds! The next thing to do is to pray and invite God in. Ask Him for clarity, peace, and victory over your anxiety, in your own words.

We take the first step to overcoming anxiety when we start shifting our minds from uncertainty (anxious and obsessive thoughts) to what is certain (God's goodness and sovereignty). Philippians 4 verse 8 (NIV) says, "Finally, brothers and sisters, whatever is true, whatever is noble, whatever is right, whatever is pure, whatever is lovely, whatever is admirable—if anything is excellent or praiseworthy—think about such things." So when anxious "what if" thoughts try to take the spotlight (and they will certainly try), choose to intentionally "think about such things" and fill your mind with Scripture and God's truth instead!

When you feel shook, like you can't see the way out of a problem, your thoughts are spiraling down fast, or you don't know what the future holds, PREACH to your soul what God says about you and about who He is. Anxiety says, "what if..." but God's peace says, "even if!"

If your thoughts say, "yeah, but what if [worst case scenario] happens?" tell yourself, "EVEN IF that was to happen, God will be with me and won't forsake me." Remind yourself of Isaiah 43:2 (NIV): "When you pass through the waters, I will be with you; and when you pass through the rivers, they will not sweep over you. When you walk through the fire, you will not be burned; the flames will not set you ablaze."

If your thoughts say, "what if [something you're hoping for] doesn't happen or is messed up?" then encourage yourself, "EVEN IF things don't work out the way I hoped, God has a plan for me, and He can turn this around for my good." Remember what Jeremiah 29:11 (NIV) says, "For I know the plans I have for you," declares the Lord, "plans to prosper you and not to harm you, plans to give you hope and a future."

Use these and any of your favorite verses to focus on how faithful and mighty God is. When you make room for what's true and good, your mind has no room for anxiety! Let's do what 2 Corinthians 10 verse 5 (NIV) says: "take captive every thought to make it obedient to Christ." So give anxiety an eviction letter, and remind it that your mind is God's home!

PRAYER FOR TODAY

Dear God, thank you for giving us the key to overcoming anxiety with your truth and presence. Please teach me how to take hold of my anxious thoughts and preach your truth to my soul. Holy Spirit, remind me of Scripture and speak truth to my mind. Regardless of what the future holds, today I believe that you have good plans for me, and I choose not to fear. I choose to trust your Word when it says that you will be with me through the waters and the fire.

In Jesus' name, amen.

19

FINDING JOY IN ANXIOUS SEASONS

NATHALIE MAXEY

So far we've covered acknowledging our anxiety, praying and inviting God into our journey, and preaching to our soul about God's truth and goodness. Today's topic is one of my favorite ones! It's one of those hard lessons in life that take some time to "get," but once you realize it, you can't live without it. Today, we'll be talking about finding JOY in spite of anxiety!

Rejoice in the Lord always. I will say it again: Rejoice!

PHILIPPIANS 4:4 (NIV)

The past three days we covered verses 6-8 of Philippians 4 (NIV), and today I want to go back to verse 4. It tells us to "Rejoice in the Lord always. I will say it again: Rejoice!" right before we're called to "not be anxious about anything" (verse 6, NIV). When life is good, it's easy to have joy, isn't it? It's those other difficult moments where questions like "Why me? When will it end? Why do they have it better than me? Why now?" cloud our minds and fill us with anxiety!

Knowing brokenness from a young age, I lived in "survival mode" (barely getting by) most of my life. I used to look at "happy people" and think, 'how are

THEY so happy?' I would read the Bible, like verse 4, and wonder HOW could I truly have joy and not be anxious all the time. Then something changed in me when I found this thing called "unconditional gratitude." Last year, when my chronic illness took over, there wasn't much to feel thankful for. Did I have health? No. Social life? No. Travel? No. Fun? No. It was at that low moment when I felt God say, "Go back to the basics. Even in this painful time, LOOK for the good. Look for what you DO have or have experienced thus far, and give me thanks for that - no matter how 'insignificant' it may seem!" So I did just that. I started to thank Him for the small wins in my day. "God, thanks that I am alive and I have a family who loves me. Thank you that I am safe in my home." Then as my health progressed, I'd say, "Thank you that today I was able to sleep without the need of freezing towels and ice packs. Thank you that I can eat a little more food. Thank you that I was able to hold my kids today."

Having gratitude over the little things unlocked true joy in my life. And guess what? As I filled my mind with "thank yous" and God's truth (as we covered yesterday), anxiety started to lose its power over me! It's why I believe that 1 Thessalonians 5:16-18 (NIV) has joy, prayer, and thanksgiving together: "Rejoice always, pray continually, give thanks in all circumstances." When your anxiety wants you to focus on what you don't have or the things that could go wrong, gratefulness speaks God's goodness and mercy over your life—which then releases joy!

So, let me leave you with this, gal—when you live in gratitude, joy follows, and then there is no room for anxiety! As you go through your day, practice Psalm 103 verse 2 (NIV), "Praise the Lord, my soul, and forget not all his benefits;" give thanks in your head or in a journal, and praise God for all that He has done throughout your life! The more you replace your anxious thoughts with ones of thanksgiving and worship, the more joy will be unlocked!

PRAYER FOR TODAY

Dear God, today I want to raise my Ebenezer and just give you thanks for bringing me this far. Thank you for dying for me on the cross and forgiving my sins. Thank you for all the times that you have helped me and rescued me. Thank you for your blessings and mercy over my life. Thank you for being my peace and my joy, no matter what I experience in this world! In Jesus' name, amen.

20

DEFEATING ANXIETY IS A JOURNEY, NOT A DESTINATION

NATHALIE MAXEY

Boom. We made it to the last day of this whole study! I am truly honored and grateful to have spent the past five days with you. I have shared some key truths and practical steps to overcome anxiety, and I want to leave you with one of the most important things: defeating anxiety is a journey, not a destination! It's a muscle that we need to work out as we grow closer in our dependency on God and practice gratefulness and joy over our anxiety!

Whatever you have learned or received or heard from me,
or seen in me—put it into practice. And the God of peace will be with you.

PHILIPPIANS 4:9 (NIV)

Do you know that satisfying feeling when you fix something or check an item off your checklist? When I realized that I had anxiety, I tried to learn everything about it; I wanted to find a book that said, "once you overcome anxiety, you will NEVER have it again." However, the more I read about it and turned to God for answers, I realized that for some of us with anxiety based on our genetics, family history, or past trauma, anxiety is not a "once and for all" or "x-marks-the-spot" type of thing. Yes, God is powerful to do miracles (so let's pray for that), but also be aware that it may be His will for you to GROW THROUGH it!

James 1 verse 2 says that we should "consider it pure joy" when we "face trials of many kinds" because it stretches our faith. Sometimes God allows us to go through anxious moments, not because He wants us to struggle, but His ultimate goal is to grow our dependence on Him and to make us more like Him! When my body was shutting down last year, I had questions and fears, but I also had this sense that there was purpose through that trial! I had "Refiner" by Maverick City Music on repeat, and my prayer changed from "God, make this stop" to "God, refine me through this fire." That shift in my soul told my anxiety "there's no room for you here," and God's peace started to give me rest even in the darkest nights!

You see, when something triggers our anxiety, we must remember to go back to offense mode! Verse 9 in Philippians 4 (NIV) says, "Whatever you have learned or received or heard from me, or seen in me—put it into practice. And the God of peace will be with you." It's not just about understanding our anxiety. The key to defeating anxiety is PRACTICING what we learned together! When anxious thoughts start to brew, stop them quickly with God's Word, thanksgiving, and worship. If they come back, stop anxiety's lies with God's truth again! It may feel like you're playing "whack-a-mole," but you're certainly strong enough to overcome it with God's help!

So, gal, as we finish our study, please know that you're not alone in your anxiety journey! 2 Corinthians 1:3-4 (NIV) says that God comforts us "so that we can comfort those in any trouble with the comfort we ourselves receive from God." If God can help me overcome anxiety (especially after 2020), I know that he can do it for you! So, take heart because there is HOPE! You too can defeat anxiety and learn to live a life that says, "EVEN IF life doesn't go my way, I know that I can have peace because God's got me!"

PRAYER FOR TODAY

Dear Father, I praise you and worship you for who you are.
Thank you for creating me fearfully and wonderfully, with
purpose and hope. I may not understand everything I'm going
through, but I choose to trust in your perfect and good will for
my life. I know that you're going ahead of me so I don't have
to worry about tomorrow. Today, I declare that anxiety no
longer has a hold of my life, and I ask for your joy and peace
that transcends all understanding to guard my mind and soul.
When anxiety tries to overwhelm me again, give me the clarity
and strength to "whack it" with your truth. I know that you are
bigger than my anxiety, and with your help I will overcome it!

In Jesus' name, amen.

Toni Collier

TONI COLLIER is the founder of an international women's ministry called Broken Crayons Still Color, which helps women process through brokenness and get to hope. She serves alongside her husband, Sam, who is the Lead Pastor of Hillsong Atlanta. She is a speaker, host, and consultant that has helped organizations with creative marketing, leadership, student ministry, and strategic planning. Toni is teaching people all over the globe that you can be broken and worthy and unqualified and still called to do great things. She doesn't want you to just face your demons, she wants you to quash the illusion of your brokenness so you can live the most colorful life possible, on and off stage.

Hope Moquin

HOPE MOQUIN is the Associate Director at Free Chapel College and founder of Becoming Better, a mentorship program that equips women to become the woman they know they are called to be. Her mission is to help women use what they have experienced for good and commit to a pursuit of becoming better in every area of life. She is a speaker, author and life coach that believes in celebrating people and inspiring people to live for Jesus.

Sewa Fields

SEWA FIELDS is the Community Engagement Specialist for Broken Crayons Still Color and a Student Support Team Coordinator for the local school system. Born and raised in India, Sewa moved to the US in her adult years. Despite her sheltered upbringing, she encountered abuse and loss through her adult years that eventually led to a beautiful story of redemption and restoration. Sewa has used her story to serve and bring hope in a variety of ministry capacities with North Point Ministries and Broken Crayons Still Color.

Nathalie Maxey

NATHALIE MAXEY is a Honduran innovation designer and writer in Atlanta, Ga. After having her two sweet and energetic kiddos, she made a pivot from the web and mobile tech industry into the creative field. Her passion for technology and sharing hope now fuel her to take creative design to a new level. From multi-dimensional photography, illustrations, animations, branding, and merchandise design, Nathalie takes the heart of an organization and creates marketing that's engaging and attractive. She's helped organizations like: International Peacemaking NGO Preemptive Love, Good Grit Magazine, Broken Crayons Women's Brand, TRIBL Music, various ministries, and leaders across the country.